50 Wholesome Food Bites

By: Kelly Johnson

Table of Contents

- Avocado Toast with Cherry Tomatoes
- Roasted Chickpeas with Paprika
- Quinoa and Veggie Patties
- Veggie Spring Rolls with Peanut Sauce
- Baked Sweet Potato Fries
- Hummus with Cucumber and Carrot Sticks
- Energy Bites with Oats and Almond Butter
- Cauliflower Buffalo Bites
- Greek Yogurt with Honey and Walnuts
- Roasted Brussels Sprouts with Lemon
- Baked Zucchini Chips
- Spinach and Feta Stuffed Mushrooms
- Roasted Almonds with Sea Salt
- Mini Egg Salad Sandwiches
- Grilled Veggie Skewers
- Sliced Apple with Peanut Butter
- Sweet Potato and Black Bean Tacos

- Chia Pudding with Mixed Berries
- Roasted Garlic and Herb Popcorn
- Fresh Fruit Salad with Lime
- Mini Veggie Burgers
- Overnight Oats with Almond Milk
- Baked Falafel with Tzatziki
- Sweet Potato Hummus
- Veggie and Cheese Quesadillas
- Cucumber and Cream Cheese Bites
- Cabbage and Carrot Slaw
- Grilled Chicken Skewers with Lemon
- Cucumber and Avocado Sushi Rolls
- Veggie-Stuffed Mini Bell Peppers
- Smashed Avocado on Rice Cakes
- Mini Quiche with Spinach and Cheese
- Banana and Almond Butter Sandwiches
- Stuffed Grape Leaves with Rice
- Rice Paper Rolls with Shrimp and Veggies
- Baked Eggplant Parmesan Bites

- Coconut and Date Energy Balls
- Grilled Halloumi with Lemon
- Sweet Corn and Black Bean Salad
- Broccoli and Cheddar Bites
- Quinoa Salad with Lemon Dressing
- Edamame with Sea Salt
- Mango Salsa with Tortilla Chips
- Carrot and Celery Sticks with Ranch Dip
- Roasted Beets with Goat Cheese
- Apple and Cheese Skewers
- Mini Avocado and Tomato Toasts
- Sweet Potato and Chickpea Curry Bites
- Cucumber and Avocado Salad
- Mini Caprese Skewers with Balsamic Glaze

Avocado Toast with Cherry Tomatoes

- Ingredients:

    1. 2 slices whole grain bread, toasted
    2. 1 ripe avocado
    3. 1/2 cup cherry tomatoes, halved
    4. Salt and pepper to taste
    5. Drizzle of olive oil

- Instructions:

    1. Mash avocado and spread onto toasted bread.
    2. Top with cherry tomatoes, salt, pepper, and a drizzle of olive oil.
    3. Serve immediately.

Roasted Chickpeas with Paprika

- Ingredients:

    1. 1 can chickpeas, drained and rinsed
    2. 1 tbsp olive oil
    3. 1 tsp smoked paprika
    4. 1/2 tsp garlic powder
    5. Salt to taste

- Instructions:

    1. Preheat oven to 400°F (200°C).
    2. Pat chickpeas dry and toss with oil and seasonings.
    3. Roast for 25-30 minutes, shaking halfway through, until crispy.

Quinoa and Veggie Patties

- Ingredients:

    1. 1 cup cooked quinoa

    2. 1/2 cup grated carrot

    3. 1/2 cup chopped spinach

    4. 1 egg

    5. 1/4 cup breadcrumbs

    6. Salt and pepper to taste

- Instructions:

    1. Mix all ingredients in a bowl.

    2. Form into patties.

    3. Cook in a lightly oiled skillet over medium heat until golden, about 4 minutes per side.

Veggie Spring Rolls with Peanut Sauce

- Ingredients:

    1. 8 rice paper wrappers
    2. 1 cup shredded carrots
    3. 1 cup shredded cabbage
    4. 1 cucumber, julienned
    5. 1/2 cup fresh mint or basil
    6. For sauce: 1/4 cup peanut butter, 1 tbsp soy sauce, 1 tbsp lime juice, water to thin

- Instructions:

    1. Soften rice paper in warm water.
    2. Fill with veggies and herbs, then roll tightly.
    3. Mix sauce ingredients and serve on the side.

Baked Sweet Potato Fries

- Ingredients:

    1. 2 sweet potatoes, peeled and cut into fries
    2. 1 tbsp olive oil
    3. 1/2 tsp paprika
    4. Salt and pepper to taste

- Instructions:

    1. Preheat oven to 425°F (220°C).
    2. Toss fries with oil and seasonings.
    3. Bake for 25-30 minutes, flipping halfway through.

Hummus with Cucumber and Carrot Sticks

- Ingredients:

    1. 1 cup hummus
    2. 1 cucumber, cut into sticks
    3. 2 carrots, cut into sticks

- Instructions:

    1. Arrange hummus in a bowl.
    2. Serve with fresh veggie sticks for dipping.

Energy Bites with Oats and Almond Butter

- Ingredients:
    1. 1 cup rolled oats
    2. 1/2 cup almond butter
    3. 1/4 cup honey or maple syrup
    4. 1/4 cup mini chocolate chips (optional)
- Instructions:
    1. Mix all ingredients in a bowl.
    2. Roll into bite-sized balls.
    3. Chill for 30 minutes before serving.

Cauliflower Buffalo Bites

- Ingredients:

    1. 1 head cauliflower, cut into florets
    2. 1/2 cup flour
    3. 1/2 cup water
    4. 1/2 cup hot sauce
    5. 1 tbsp melted butter

- Instructions:

    1. Preheat oven to 425°F (220°C).
    2. Mix flour and water into a batter.
    3. Coat cauliflower in batter, place on baking sheet, and bake for 20 minutes.
    4. Toss baked cauliflower in hot sauce and butter, then bake 10 more minutes.

Greek Yogurt with Honey and Walnuts

- Ingredients:
    1. 1 cup plain Greek yogurt
    2. 1 tbsp honey
    3. 2 tbsp chopped walnuts
- Instructions:
    1. Spoon yogurt into a bowl.
    2. Drizzle with honey and sprinkle with walnuts.
    3. Serve chilled.

Roasted Brussels Sprouts with Lemon

- Ingredients:

    1. 1 lb Brussels sprouts, halved
    2. 2 tbsp olive oil
    3. Salt and pepper to taste
    4. Juice of 1/2 lemon

- Instructions:

    1. Preheat oven to 400°F (200°C).
    2. Toss sprouts with oil, salt, and pepper.
    3. Roast for 25-30 minutes until crispy.
    4. Squeeze lemon juice over before serving.

Baked Zucchini Chips

- Ingredients:

    1. 2 zucchinis, thinly sliced
    2. 1 tbsp olive oil
    3. 1/2 tsp sea salt

- Instructions:

    1. Preheat oven to 225°F (110°C).
    2. Toss zucchini slices in olive oil and salt.
    3. Arrange on a baking sheet and bake for 1.5–2 hours, flipping halfway, until crisp.

Spinach and Feta Stuffed Mushrooms

- Ingredients:

    1. 12 large button mushrooms, stems removed
    2. 1/2 cup cooked spinach, chopped
    3. 1/4 cup crumbled feta cheese
    4. 1 clove garlic, minced

- Instructions:

    1. Preheat oven to 375°F (190°C).
    2. Mix spinach, feta, and garlic.
    3. Stuff mushrooms and bake for 20 minutes.

Roasted Almonds with Sea Salt

- Ingredients:

    1. 2 cups raw almonds
    2. 1 tbsp olive oil
    3. 1 tsp sea salt

- Instructions:

    1. Preheat oven to 350°F (175°C).
    2. Toss almonds with olive oil and salt.
    3. Spread on a baking sheet and roast for 12–15 minutes, stirring halfway.

Mini Egg Salad Sandwiches

- Ingredients:
    1. 4 hard-boiled eggs, chopped
    2. 2 tbsp mayonnaise
    3. Salt and pepper to taste
    4. 6 slices bread, crusts removed and halved
- Instructions:
    1. Mix eggs with mayo, salt, and pepper.
    2. Spread on bread and sandwich together.
    3. Cut into mini triangles.

Grilled Veggie Skewers

- Ingredients:

    1. 1 zucchini, sliced
    2. 1 bell pepper, chopped
    3. 1 red onion, chopped
    4. Olive oil, salt, and pepper

- Instructions:

    1. Skewer vegetables and brush with oil.
    2. Season with salt and pepper.
    3. Grill over medium heat for 8–10 minutes, turning occasionally.

Sliced Apple with Peanut Butter

- Ingredients:
    1. 1 apple, sliced
    2. 2 tbsp peanut butter
- Instructions:
    1. Arrange apple slices on a plate.
    2. Serve with peanut butter for dipping.

Sweet Potato and Black Bean Tacos

- Ingredients:

    1. 1 large sweet potato, diced
    2. 1 tbsp olive oil
    3. 1/2 tsp chili powder
    4. 1 cup black beans, drained
    5. 4 corn tortillas

- Instructions:

    1. Roast sweet potato with oil and chili powder at 400°F (200°C) for 25 minutes.
    2. Warm tortillas and fill with sweet potato and black beans.
    3. Serve with optional toppings like salsa or avocado.

Chia Pudding with Mixed Berries

- Ingredients:

    1. 1/4 cup chia seeds
    2. 1 cup almond milk
    3. 1 tsp honey or maple syrup
    4. 1/2 cup mixed berries

- Instructions:

    1. Mix chia seeds, milk, and sweetener in a jar.
    2. Refrigerate for at least 4 hours or overnight.
    3. Top with berries before serving.

Roasted Garlic and Herb Popcorn

- Ingredients:
    1. 1/2 cup popcorn kernels
    2. 2 tbsp olive oil
    3. 1/2 tsp garlic powder
    4. 1/2 tsp dried herbs (like thyme or rosemary)
    5. Salt to taste
- Instructions:
    1. Pop kernels in a popcorn maker or pot.
    2. Toss with oil, garlic powder, herbs, and salt.
    3. Serve warm.

Fresh Fruit Salad with Lime

- Ingredients:
    1. 1 cup strawberries, halved
    2. 1 cup pineapple chunks
    3. 1 cup blueberries
    4. 1 cup kiwi, sliced
    5. Juice of 1 lime
- Instructions:
    1. Combine all fruit in a large bowl.
    2. Drizzle with lime juice and toss gently.
    3. Chill before serving.

Mini Veggie Burgers

- Ingredients:
    1. 1 can black beans, mashed
    2. 1/2 cup breadcrumbs
    3. 1/4 cup grated carrot
    4. 1 egg
    5. 1/2 tsp cumin
- Instructions:
    1. Mix all ingredients and form into small patties.
    2. Cook in a skillet over medium heat, 3–4 minutes per side.
    3. Serve on mini buns with desired toppings.

Overnight Oats with Almond Milk

- Ingredients:
    1. 1/2 cup rolled oats
    2. 1/2 cup almond milk
    3. 1 tsp chia seeds
    4. 1/2 banana, sliced
- Instructions:
    1. Combine oats, milk, and chia seeds in a jar.
    2. Stir well, top with banana, and refrigerate overnight.
    3. Stir and enjoy in the morning.

Baked Falafel with Tzatziki

- Ingredients:
    1. 1 can chickpeas
    2. 1/4 cup chopped parsley
    3. 2 cloves garlic
    4. 1 tsp cumin
    5. 2 tbsp flour
- Instructions:
    1. Blend all ingredients until coarse.
    2. Form into balls and place on a baking sheet.
    3. Bake at 400°F (200°C) for 20–25 minutes.
    4. Serve with tzatziki sauce.

Sweet Potato Hummus

- Ingredients:
    1. 1 cup cooked sweet potato
    2. 1 can chickpeas
    3. 2 tbsp tahini
    4. 1 tbsp lemon juice
    5. Salt to taste
- Instructions:
    1. Blend all ingredients until smooth.
    2. Adjust seasoning and serve chilled.

Veggie and Cheese Quesadillas

- Ingredients:
    1. 2 flour tortillas
    2. 1/2 cup shredded cheese
    3. 1/4 cup bell pepper, sliced
    4. 1/4 cup spinach
- Instructions:
    1. Layer cheese and veggies on one tortilla.
    2. Top with second tortilla and cook in a skillet until golden.
    3. Cut into wedges and serve.

Cucumber and Cream Cheese Bites

- Ingredients:
    1. 1 cucumber, sliced
    2. 1/4 cup cream cheese
    3. 1 tbsp chopped dill
- Instructions:
    1. Mix cream cheese with dill.
    2. Spread on cucumber slices.
    3. Serve chilled.

Cabbage and Carrot Slaw

- Ingredients:

    1. 2 cups shredded cabbage
    2. 1 cup shredded carrot
    3. 2 tbsp apple cider vinegar
    4. 1 tbsp olive oil
    5. Salt and pepper to taste

- Instructions:

    1. Toss all ingredients in a bowl.
    2. Let sit for 10–15 minutes before serving.

Grilled Chicken Skewers with Lemon

- Ingredients:

    1. 1 lb chicken breast, cubed
    2. 2 tbsp olive oil
    3. Juice of 1 lemon
    4. 1 tsp garlic powder

- Instructions:

    1. Marinate chicken in lemon juice, oil, and garlic powder.
    2. Skewer and grill over medium heat for 10–12 minutes, turning occasionally.

Cucumber and Avocado Sushi Rolls

- Ingredients:
    1. 1 cup cooked sushi rice
    2. 1 nori sheet
    3. 1/4 avocado, sliced
    4. 1/4 cucumber, julienned
- Instructions:
    1. Spread rice on nori sheet.
    2. Add avocado and cucumber.
    3. Roll tightly, slice, and serve with soy sauce.

Veggie-Stuffed Mini Bell Peppers

- Ingredients:

    1. 10 mini bell peppers, halved and deseeded
    2. 1/2 cup hummus or cream cheese
    3. 1/4 cup diced cucumber
    4. 1/4 cup shredded carrots

- Instructions:

    1. Fill each pepper half with hummus or cream cheese.
    2. Top with cucumber and carrot.
    3. Serve immediately or chill before serving.

Smashed Avocado on Rice Cakes

- Ingredients:

    1. 2 rice cakes

    2. 1 ripe avocado

    3. Salt, pepper, and red pepper flakes

- Instructions:

    1. Mash avocado in a bowl and season.

    2. Spread over rice cakes.

    3. Top with red pepper flakes if desired.

Mini Quiche with Spinach and Cheese

- Ingredients:

    1. 4 eggs
    2. 1/4 cup milk
    3. 1/2 cup chopped spinach
    4. 1/4 cup shredded cheese

- Instructions:

    1. Preheat oven to 375°F (190°C).
    2. Mix all ingredients and pour into mini muffin tins.
    3. Bake for 15–20 minutes until set.

Banana and Almond Butter Sandwiches

- Ingredients:

    1. 1 banana, sliced
    2. 2 tbsp almond butter
    3. 2 slices whole grain bread

- Instructions:

    1. Spread almond butter on bread.
    2. Layer banana slices and top with second slice.
    3. Cut and serve.

Stuffed Grape Leaves with Rice

- Ingredients:
    1. 1 jar grape leaves
    2. 1 cup cooked rice
    3. 1/4 cup chopped parsley
    4. Juice of 1 lemon
- Instructions:
    1. Mix rice, parsley, and lemon juice.
    2. Roll a spoonful into each grape leaf.
    3. Chill before serving.

Rice Paper Rolls with Shrimp and Veggies

- Ingredients:
    1. 6 rice paper wrappers
    2. 12 cooked shrimp, halved
    3. 1/2 cup shredded lettuce
    4. 1/2 cup julienned carrot and cucumber
- Instructions:
    1. Soften rice paper in warm water.
    2. Layer shrimp and veggies.
    3. Roll tightly and serve with dipping sauce.

Baked Eggplant Parmesan Bites

- Ingredients:

    1. 1 eggplant, sliced into rounds
    2. 1/2 cup marinara sauce
    3. 1/4 cup shredded mozzarella
    4. 2 tbsp grated parmesan

- Instructions:

    1. Preheat oven to 400°F (200°C).
    2. Bake eggplant rounds 10 minutes per side.
    3. Top with sauce and cheese and bake 5 more minutes.

Coconut and Date Energy Balls

- Ingredients:

    1. 1 cup pitted dates
    2. 1/2 cup shredded coconut
    3. 1/4 cup oats

- Instructions:

    1. Blend all ingredients in a food processor.
    2. Roll into small balls.
    3. Chill for 30 minutes before serving.

Grilled Halloumi with Lemon

- Ingredients:

    1. 8 oz halloumi cheese, sliced
    2. 1 tbsp olive oil
    3. Juice of 1 lemon

- Instructions:

    1. Heat grill or skillet and brush halloumi with oil.
    2. Grill 2–3 minutes per side.
    3. Drizzle with lemon juice before serving.

Sweet Corn and Black Bean Salad

- Ingredients:

    1. 1 cup corn kernels
    2. 1 cup black beans, drained
    3. 1/4 cup chopped red onion
    4. Juice of 1 lime

- Instructions:

    1. Combine all ingredients in a bowl.
    2. Mix well and chill before serving.

Broccoli and Cheddar Bites

- Ingredients:
    1. 1 cup steamed broccoli, finely chopped
    2. 1/2 cup shredded cheddar cheese
    3. 1/4 cup breadcrumbs
    4. 1 egg
- Instructions:
    1. Preheat oven to 375°F (190°C).
    2. Mix all ingredients in a bowl.
    3. Form into small balls and place on a baking sheet.
    4. Bake for 15–20 minutes until golden.

Quinoa Salad with Lemon Dressing

- Ingredients:

    1. 1 cup cooked quinoa
    2. 1/2 cup chopped cucumber
    3. 1/2 cup cherry tomatoes, halved
    4. 2 tbsp chopped parsley
    5. Juice of 1 lemon

- Instructions:

    1. Combine quinoa, veggies, and parsley in a bowl.
    2. Drizzle with lemon juice and toss well.
    3. Chill before serving.

Edamame with Sea Salt

- Ingredients:
    1. 1 cup edamame in pods
    2. 1/2 tsp sea salt
- Instructions:
    1. Boil edamame for 3–4 minutes.
    2. Drain and sprinkle with sea salt.
    3. Serve warm.

Mango Salsa with Tortilla Chips

- Ingredients:
    1. 1 ripe mango, diced
    2. 1/4 cup red onion, finely chopped
    3. 1 tbsp chopped cilantro
    4. Juice of 1 lime
- Instructions:
    1. Mix mango, onion, and cilantro in a bowl.
    2. Add lime juice and toss.
    3. Serve with tortilla chips.

Carrot and Celery Sticks with Ranch Dip

- Ingredients:

    1. 1 cup carrot sticks
    2. 1 cup celery sticks
    3. 1/2 cup ranch dressing

- Instructions:

    1. Arrange carrot and celery sticks on a plate.
    2. Serve with a side of ranch dressing.

Roasted Beets with Goat Cheese

- Ingredients:

    1. 2 medium beets, peeled and diced
    2. 1 tbsp olive oil
    3. 1/4 cup goat cheese, crumbled

- Instructions:

    1. Preheat oven to 400°F (200°C).
    2. Toss beets with olive oil and roast for 25–30 minutes.
    3. Cool slightly and top with goat cheese.

Apple and Cheese Skewers

- Ingredients:
    1. 1 apple, cubed
    2. 1/2 cup cheddar cheese, cubed
    3. Small skewers or toothpicks

- Instructions:
    1. Thread apple and cheese cubes alternately on skewers.
    2. Serve immediately or refrigerate.

Mini Avocado and Tomato Toasts

- Ingredients:

    1. 1 ripe avocado
    2. 6 cherry tomatoes, halved
    3. 6 slices baguette, toasted

- Instructions:

    1. Mash avocado and spread on toasted baguette slices.
    2. Top with cherry tomato halves.
    3. Season with salt and pepper if desired.

Sweet Potato and Chickpea Curry Bites

- Ingredients:

    1. 1 cup cooked mashed sweet potato
    2. 1/2 cup cooked chickpeas, mashed
    3. 1 tsp curry powder

- Instructions:

    1. Mix all ingredients together.
    2. Form into small patties and pan-fry until golden.
    3. Serve warm or at room temperature.

Cucumber and Avocado Salad

- Ingredients:
    1. 1 cucumber, diced
    2. 1 ripe avocado, diced
    3. Juice of 1 lime
- Instructions:
    1. Toss cucumber and avocado in a bowl.
    2. Add lime juice and mix gently.
    3. Chill before serving.

Mini Caprese Skewers with Balsamic Glaze

- Ingredients:
    1. 12 cherry tomatoes
    2. 12 mini mozzarella balls
    3. 12 fresh basil leaves
    4. Balsamic glaze

- Instructions:
    1. Thread one tomato, one mozzarella ball, and one basil leaf on each skewer.
    2. Drizzle with balsamic glaze before serving.

www.ingramcontent.com/pod-product-compliance
Lightning Source LLC
LaVergne TN
LVHW081329060526
838201LV00055B/2545